Grimm's Fairy Tales

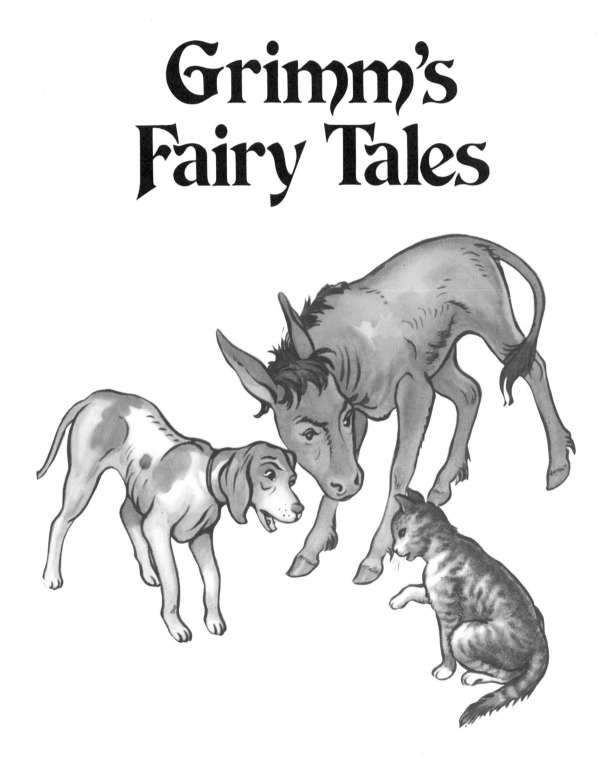

Published in the United States and Canada by
Joshua Morris Publishing, Inc.
221 Danbury Road
Wilton, Connecticut 06897

Printed in Hong Kong

The nine classic Grimm's
tales retold in this edition:

Hansel and Gretel

Once there was a poor woodcutter who had a wife and two children, Hansel and Gretel. One day he said to his wife, "How can we feed the children when we do not even have food for ourselves!"

"I'll tell you," answered the wife who was only the children's stepmother. "We will take them into the woods and then go about our work and leave them there. They will never find their way home."

"What will we do?" Gretel cried, having overheard her stepmother.

"I will think of something," Hansel said.

At dawn, the stepmother came to wake them. "We

are going into the forest to fetch wood," she told
them. "Here is some bread for your dinner."

All the way into the forest Hansel dropped crumbs
of his bread.

When they were deep in the woods, their father said, "Now build a fire and rest while we go chop some wood." The children sat by the fire and when dinner time came, Gretel shared her bread with

Hansel. The children waited so long for their father and stepmother to return that they finally fell asleep. When they woke up it was dark and they were alone. When the moon rose, they looked for Hansel's path of crumbs, not knowing that the birds had eaten every one. Hansel and Gretel were all alone and lost. They wandered for three days, frightened and hungry until they

came to a clearing where they saw a house more wonderful than anything they had ever dreamed. It was made of gingerbread and candy. Gretel began to eat a piece of the roof while Hansel nibbled hungrily at a shingle.

"I wish we had a house just like this one. I wonder how it ever came to be here," Gretel said.

All of a sudden, the door opened and an old woman hobbled out. "Do not be afraid," she said. "No harm will come to you. I don't get many visitors out here in the woods." She took the children inside and made them a delicious dinner and gave them two cozy beds. Hansel and Gretel crept beneath the sheets and felt as if they were in Heaven.

The two children had not realized that the old woman

was really a witch who had built the candy house just to lure children to her. Whenever she captured one, she cooked him and ate him for a great feast.

Early the next morning the old woman grabbed

Hansel and locked him in a cage. She woke Gretel and told her to go and cook something to fatten her brother up so she could eat him. Poor Gretel cried and cried, but it was no use.

Every morning the old woman would hobble out to the cage and demand to feel Hansel's finger to see if he was fat enough yet. However her eyesight was poor and Hansel tricked her by sticking a bone through the bars.

After a few weeks the witch lost patience and could wait no longer. "Now, Gretel," she said, "fetch water for the cauldron, for fat or thin, I shall eat Hansel." Tears streamed down Gretel's face as she went to the well. The witch made Gretel fill the kettle and start the fire. "First we will bake bread," she said. "Crawl into the oven and see if the fire is hot enough." She meant to close the child in the oven, but Gretel guessed her plan.

"Oh, I'd never fit," she said. "You stupid goose," the witch cried. "See, I could fit in myself." Quickly Gretel gave the witch a push, shoving her right into the oven, slamming the iron door and bolting it shut. Gretel ran to free Hansel. The children

were so happy. With nothing to fear, they looked about the witch's house and found pearls, precious jewels and gold coins. They filled their pockets and quickly left.

They soon came to a river which they could not cross. But a beautiful duck came and helped the children, one by one, to the other side. The forest

16

there was more familiar and, at last, Hansel and
Gretel saw their father's house. They rushed to him.
When the poor man saw the pearls and jewels he
knew all their troubles were over.

17

Snow White

Once upon a time there was a lovely Princess named Snow White. Her stepmother, the Queen, was very beautiful. But she was also proud and jealous of anyone who might match her beauty.

The Queen had magical powers and a strange magic mirror on her wall. Facing the mirror every day, she asked anxiously, "Mirror, mirror, on the wall, who is the fairest of us all?" And each day the mirror would reply, "You are the fairest one of all. No one is more beautiful than you." However one day the mirror answered, "Snow White is now the fairest one of all."

"She must die," cried the envious, evil Queen. Trembling with rage, she called out for one of

her huntsmen and commanded him to take Snow
White into the forest and kill her. But the huntsman
could not do this. Instead he took Snow White into
the deepest woods and told her to hide. Alone and

frightened, Snow White wandered through the forest until she came upon a little cottage in a clearing. Inside she was surprised to find seven little chairs set at a little table piled high with the morning's

20

dishes. Upstairs there were seven little beds and, seeing them, she felt so tired, she laid down and fell right to sleep. When the Seven Dwarfs who lived there came home from working in the mines, they were amazed to discover Snow White.

"Who can she be?" they asked each other. The kind little men waited patiently until she awoke and then they listened sadly while she told her story.

Then the oldest said, "If you will cook and clean our house, you can stay here."

"Oh, thank you," Snow White said, and the Seven Dwarfs' house became her home.

Every day the dwarfs went off to work and left Snow White alone. Afraid that the wicked Queen might find her, they warned Snow White never to let anyone into the house. Snow White promised her new friends that she wouldn't. She was content, happily taking care of their cottage.

The Queen, though, was not content. For whenever she stood before her mirror and asked, "Mirror, mirror on the wall, who is the fairest of us all?" the mirror replied, "Over seven hills where seven dwarfs dwell, Snow White is there alive and well." The Queen knew then that the huntsman had not obeyed her. Filled with hatred and jealousy, she set out to kill Snow White. Using her evil magic, she created an irresistible apple, actually poisonous and deadly. Disguising herself as an old peddler

woman, she filled a basket with apples and hurried into the woods to find Snow White.

When the Queen called to Snow White at the window of the little cottage, Snow White was cautious

at first. "I am sorry," she said. "I cannot buy your apples or let you in."

"But," pleaded the evil Queen, "I want you to have this beautiful, red apple," and she held it out to Snow White. Snow White could not resist and biting into the poisonous apple, she fell to the ground.

The Seven Dwarfs wept with grief when they found their beautiful Snow White. She was so lovely they placed her in a glass case and one of them always watched over her. Snow White rested there a long time, remaining as pretty as the day they found her.

One day, a handsome Prince came though the forest and, seeing Snow White, fell deeply in love with her. He begged the dwarfs to let him take her back to his kingdom. Finally, they agreed. When they moved the glass case, the piece of poisoned apple fell from Snow White's mouth. Suddenly, she opened her eyes and moved. Snow White was alive! Everyone was overcome with joy! The Prince held out his hand to Snow White and helped her up. "Oh, what a lovely rest," she said, looking around her.

Soon after, Snow White and the Prince were married and the Seven Dwarfs danced and danced at the wedding celebration. Snow White was happy and so were they.

The Wolf and Seven Kids

There once was a nanny goat who had seven kids and she loved them as much as any mother loves her childen. One day she was going into the woods to fetch some food and she called them together and said, "My dear children, while I am away, beware of the wolf! He is clever and may disguise himself, but you will know him by his rough voice and his black feet!"

The kids listened well and told their mother, "Do not worry, for we will be very careful." So the nanny goat went off to the forest.

Before long, someone knocked at the door and called, "Open the door, children, it is your mother. I have come back with a surprise for each of you."

But the children knew right away by the voice that it was the wolf and they cried, "No, no, we will not open the door for you. You are not our mother. Our mother has a soft, gentle voice and yours is deep and rough."

So the crafty wolf went away to think about what to do next. Suddenly he had a wonderful idea! He ate some honey, which softened his voice. He then returned to the house and again he knocked at the door and called, "Open the door, dear children. It is your mother. I have come back with a surprise for each of you."

But as he spoke, he put one of his paws on the windowsill and the kids could see it there. "No, no, you are not our mother," they cried. "Our mother does not have black feet, but you do! You are the wolf! We will not let you in."

Angry, the cunning wolf ran to the baker. "I have hurt my feet," he said. "You must put some dough on them." And so the baker did. Then the wolf ran to the miller and commanded, "Dust my feet with flour." The miller suspected that the wolf was up to some trick, and he refused. But the wolf said, "I will eat you up if you do not!" And so the miller dusted the wolf's feet. Now the wicked wolf rushed back to the house, knocked on the door again and called, "Open the door, dear children. It is your mother come home from the woods and I have

brought you something that you will love."

The kids cried, "If you are our mother, show us your feet!" So he put his paws on the windowsill and the children, seeing his feet whitened by the dough and flour, believed him. And so they opened the door.

When the kids saw the wolf, they were terrified and they ran everywhere trying to hide. One kid ran under the table, another jumped into the bed and a third hid in the oven. The fourth fled to the kitchen, the fifth climbed into the cupboard and the sixth ducked into the washtub. The last little kid closed himself into the clockcase. The wolf, with his sharp nose and quick claws, had no trouble catching the little kids and he speedily swallowed up everyone except the youngest kid, who stayed hidden and frightened in the clockcase.

Having eaten greedily, the wretched wolf went to a nearby meadow, lay down and fell quickly into a deep sleep.

Not long afterwards, the mother returned home from the woods. When she saw the door open, she knew something was wrong. When she saw the tables and chairs overturned and the bed torn apart, she searched for her children in horror. She called each of their names, but no one answered.

Finally, the youngest kid, still hidden in the clockcase, called out, "Here I am mother, here I

am! Over here in the clockcase. Please come and get me out." She took him out and he tearfully told her how the wolf had come and eaten all the others.

The nanny goat, hugging her youngest kid to her very tightly, wept and wept over her lost children. Full of sorrow, she took her youngest kid by the hand and she went down to the meadow to sit among the beautiful flowers and think about her lost children who were so good. There she discovered the hideous

wolf laying under a tree snoring noisily. She and the little kid looked closely at him. The mother goat thought hopefully, "Maybe my children are in his stomach and still alive!" Quickly she put the little kid on the wolf's stomach. She then told him to jump up and down on his stomach while she held the wolf's mouth wide open. All of a sudden, one little kid popped out. And that one was quickly followed by another and then another and another, until all six children were with her again. They all jumped eagerly into their mother's arms. Each was alive and unharmed, for the greedy wolf had swallowed them whole.

The nanny goat rejoiced and hugged and kissed each little kid and she told them never, ever to let anyone in the house again when she was not there.

The little kids promised. And then they filled the wolf's stomach with stones that they had gathered. This way they made certain that he would never again be able to run after them or catch them.

At last, happy to be together and safe from harm, they all linked arms and danced and danced for joy.

Little Red Riding Hood

Once upon a time there was a sweet little girl who always wore a red cape and hood. And so she was called Little Red Riding Hood.

One day her mother called her and said, "Take this basket of food to Grandmother. She is not well and this will make her feel better. Go straight through the woods. Do not stop and do not speak to any strangers."

"I will do just what you say," answered Little Red Riding Hood. And off she skipped, happy at the thought of visiting her grandmother.

Little Red Riding Hood's grandmother lived on the other side of the woods from the village. Walking along in the woods, she met a wolf. The wolf seemed friendly and the little girl, unaware of his wickedness, was not afraid.

He spoke very politely, but in his mind he had a nasty plan. "Good morning," the wolf said in a kind voice. "Where are you going on this lovely day?"

Little Red Riding Hood answered, "My grandmother is sick and I am bringing this basket of food to her to help make her well."

"Oh what a good little girl. Where does she live?" the wolf asked.

"In a little cottage near three big oak trees," Little Red Riding Hood said.

The cunning wolf was thinking that Little Red Riding Hood would make a delicious meal and he thought about eating Grandmother, too. But he said pleasantly, "Why look at all these pretty flowers. I am sure your grandmother would like to have some. Everyone loves to get fresh flowers, especially when they're feeling ill. Why don't you stop and pick some for her? I would stay and help you, but I have to be on my way."

Little Red Riding Hood, admiring the flowers, began to gather them, going farther and farther away from the path.

In the meantime, the wolf ran ahead to Grand-mother's house. He knocked on the door, but no one answered.

Grandmother had awakened that morning feeling much better and so had gone off for a long walk in the woods.

The wolf pushed open the door and walked in. He went straight to Grandmother's bedroom. There on the bed, neatly folded, was her long nightgown and nightcap. The wolf quickly put on the nightgown

and cap and hopped into bed, pulling the covers right up to his nose. He lay still, licking his chops at the thought of the fine meal ahead of him.

Meanwhile Little Red Riding Hood, her arms filled with flowers, arrived at her grandmother's house. She walked right in and called out, "Good morning, Grandmother."

"Come in, my dear," the wolf replied. "Put your basket down in the kitchen and come here so I can see you."

"Grandmother, how hoarse your voice sounds!" said Little Red Riding Hood.

"It's just a cold, my dear. But I'm not well enough to get up yet."

Little Red Riding Hood went in and put her basket in the kitchen. She went quietly up to the bed and peered closely at her grandmother who looked very strange. "Oh, Grandmother, what big ears you have," she exclaimed.

"The better to hear you with, my dear," said the crafty wolf.

"Grandmother, what big eyes you have!"

"The better to see you with, my dear."

"But, Grandmother, what big teeth you have!"

"The better to eat you with, my dear," the wolf cried. And with that he sprang out of bed grabbing poor Little Red Riding Hood. But he tripped on Grandmother's gown and fell to the floor, snarling.

A huntsman passing by heard loud shouts from Grandmother's house and saw Little Red Riding Hood running out the door. "I must go and see if I can help," he thought.

"Aha, that is the wolf that has been stealing all our lambs and breaking down our chicken coops." The huntsman shot the wolf and dragged him out the front door.

When Grandmother came home they all sat down and ate all the delicious food. Little Red Riding Hood knew then that she would never again talk to strangers or stop on the way to Grandmother's house.

The Magic Table

Once upon a time there was a tailor who had three sons—Long-Legged Michael, Fat Frank and Foolish John. He also had a goat that he was very fond of. The goat lived in the barn and was kept mainly to provide milk for the family. But in order to provide milk, the goat had to be well fed. Each day one of the boys in turn took the goat to the pasture.

One day, when Long-Legged Michael took the goat out to pasture, the boy fell asleep under a tree while the goat roamed about the meadows, filling her stomach with leaves and grass. At the end of the day, Michael asked the goat, "Did you have enough to eat? Are you full?"

"Oh yes," the goat answered. "I've had plenty to eat, thank you. I don't want anything else."

But that night, when the father asked whether she had eaten enough, the goat lied. "How can I have eaten enough when I didn't find one little leaf?" she whined miserably.

The tailor turned in anger to Long-Legged Michael. "How can you be so lazy and cruel to take this poor goat out to graze and then just go to sleep without making sure she had enough food?" The young man admitted that he had fallen asleep but he insisted that the goat had eaten well. But his father, too angry to see the truth, sent his son away from home.

Fat Frank was tricked by the crafty animal, too. After spending a day in the pasture with Frank and eating as much as she possibly could, the goat complained pitifully that she had not found a single thing to satisfy her hunger. Again the tailor believed the mischievous goat and angrily sent his second son away from home. Foolish John, the youngest son, met the same fate as his brothers.

From then on the tailor cared for the goat himself and took her to the best places to feed. He was delighted to see his animal eating the tenderest grass and the sweetest leaves and felt himself getting angry all over again at the thought of his three sons not taking proper care of the goat.

For a while, the goat was content. But one night, the ungrateful beast complained to the tailor that she had not found a decent morsel to eat all day. This time the tailor knew that the goat was lying. He had been with the goat out in the meadow and had seen her eating the tender grass and leaves.

He then realized that his sons were not to blame. The goat had tricked them all. He felt ashamed and he regretted that he had sent his sons away. Sadly, he wished, with all his heart, that they would come home again. But it was too late. Each of the boys had traveled his separate way.

Left alone and filled with rage, the tailor turned

his anger to the sly animal who tricked him. "You are the cause of all my sorrow!" he shouted at the faithless goat. "My sons would still be here if it were not for you!" Then he raised his whip furiously, cracked it in the air right above the goat's head and he chased the miserable creature away for good.

As a matter of fact, Long-Legged Michael was

working as an apprentice to a carpenter. He learned his trade easily and pleased his master with his effort and talent. When his training was completed, Michael wanted to return home. He missed his brothers and wanted to see his father, too. His master was so happy with the young man's work that he wanted to give him a farewell present. And so the carpenter gave Long-Legged Michael a little table.

"Listen well, Michael," the carpenter said. "This is a magic table. When you tell the table to get set, it will instantly serve you the most delicious foods."

Michael was amazed and grateful. He thanked his master politely and set out for home, carrying the table on his back.

On his way, he spent the night at an inn. When he arrived he didn't ask for anything to eat or drink. He just took the little table to his room and shut the door.

The innkeeper, a cunning and curious man, peeked through the keyhole. To his surprise, he saw the table set itself with the tastiest food and the finest wines. "Oh, my," he thought greedily, "I must have that table." That night he crept into the room and stole the magic table leaving an ordinary one in its place.

When Michael returned home his father was over-joyed. A big party was planned. Naturally, Michael wanted the magic table to prepare a grand feast. And although he told the table to set out the food over and over again, nothing happened. Michael stood there foolishly as his friends laughed and laughed. How could they believe that a table set itself? He

knew then that the innkeeper had tricked him.

In the meantime, the second son, Fat Frank, was an apprentice to a miller. And as soon as he completed his work, he, too, wanted to return to his father. The kind miller gave him a miraculous donkey as a farewell present.

"Tell the donkey to stretch his neck," the miller explained, "and gold coins will pour from his mouth."

Frank was amazed and thrilled. He thanked the miller and set out for home riding his magic donkey. But he had to spend one night at the inn, too. And while he slept, the sly innkeeper stole his golden donkey.

The next day, Frank rode home on an ordinary donkey unaware of what he had lost. When he tried to show his father what his marvelous donkey could do, nothing happened and Frank knew that the innkeeper had tricked him, too.

Now the youngest son, Foolish John, became a turner by trade. And when he was leaving to go home, his master gave him a precious sack.

"Just shout, 'Stick, come out of the sack,' and you will always be helped," his master explained.

On the way home, Foolish John spent the night at the same inn. When the greedy innkeeper saw the sack, he thought, "That must be filled with magic and I must have it!"

But John had heard about his brothers' bad luck, so he went to sleep with the sack under his head, guarding it carefully. When the innkeeper slipped into his room, John lay still pretending to be asleep.

And when the wicked man tried to pull the sack out from beneath him, John raised his head and shouted, "Stick, come out of the sack!" The stick flew from the sack and began to pound the innkeeper.

The man screamed for help, but no one came. He begged for mercy, but John only wanted two things—the table and the donkey. The greedy inn-keeper pleaded and even offered John money, but

finally he gave in. So John set out with the magic sack, the donkey and the table. When he arrived home his father and brothers were delighted. This time there was truly a grand celebration. And this time, to everyone's amazement, the table set out a magical feast of roasts and fish, cakes and wines. And the donkey opened his mouth and out came enough gold coins to fill everyone's empty pockets. From that day on, joy and laughter filled the lives of Foolish John and his brothers. And they all lived together happily.

Puss in Boots

Once there was a miller who, when he was very old, gave all he had to his three sons. He left the mill to his oldest son. He left the donkey to his second son. But to his youngest son, he left only the cat, Puss.

The young son was very disappointed. "How can I possibly make my way in the world with nothing but this cat?" he asked.

But Puss said, "Make me a pair of boots and get me a sack with a strong cord and you will never be unhappy again!"

When the miller's son gave Puss a fine pair of red leather boots and a sack with a good strong cord, Puss headed for the briar patch where the rabbits lived. There he filled his sack with carrots and hid behind a tree with the cord in his hand. Soon a rabbit came along and hopped right into the sack. Puss yanked the cord tightly, slung the sack over his shoulder and rushed to the King's castle.

"Your Majesty," said Puss when he stood before the King. "My master, the Marquis of Carabas, sends this rabbit to you."

"I do like fresh game," said the King gladly. "Even though I do not know the Marquis of Carabas, please thank him for me."

The next day, Puss hurried to a wheat field and filled his sack with grain. This time, a pair of partridges scurried into his trap. He pulled the cord tightly and ran to the King's castle.

"Good day, your Majesty," he said. "The Marquis of Carabas sends these birds for your pleasure." The King smiled appreciatively and sent the birds to his cooks at once.

On the third day, Puss caught two trout and again brought them to the King. Of course, the King was delighted. While at the court, Puss learned that the King was taking his daughter for a ride along the river that day.

Quickly, he ran to his master and exclaimed, "You must go for a swim in the river by the bridge today. Your fortune will be made if you do!" The miller's son was very puzzled, but he did as Puss told him, anyway. While he swam, Puss took his ragged clothes and hid them.

Soon the King's coach drove up. "Stop!" Puss yelled. "The clothes of my master, the Marquis of Carabas, have been stolen!" Remembering the delicious gifts that had been presented to him by the generous Marquis, the King sent a footman back to the castle to fetch a suit of fine clothes for him. The miller's son was amazed.

"Who is the Marquis of Carabas?" he whispered to Puss.

"You are," answered Puss and the poor lad was even more surprised. The miller's son looked very handsome in the fine clothes and he thanked the King politely for his help.

"Please join me and my daughter for a ride in my coach," the King offered. The young man accepted the kind invitation, climbed into the coach and sat down next to the lovely Princess. She looked very pleased to see him.

"Leave the rest to me," Puss whispered and he ran ahead.

Puss ran to a hay field and shouted to the workers, "When the King drives past here tell him this field belongs to the Marquis of Carabas or I will claw you to pieces!" The farmers, frightened by Puss, did as they were told. Puss ran farther ahead to a field where some reapers were working. "Reapers!" he yelled in a fierce voice. "When the King drives past tell him the Marquis of Carabas is your master."

And so they did, for Puss had scared them terribly.

Then Puss ran as fast as he could to the castle of the wicked wizard who owned these fields. When the evil wizard opened the door, Puss said, "I hear you have magical powers and I have come to pay my respect to you."

When the wizard, who was flattered, let him in Puss asked, "Is it true that you can change yourself into a huge lion?"

"Yes," he said and instantly became a fierce lion.

Then Puss slyly said, "Oh, that is wonderful. But can you change into a mouse?"

"Yes," said the wizard. And as soon as he became

a little mouse Puss pounced on him and ate him up!

When the King's beautiful coach finally arrived Puss said grandly, "Welcome to the castle of the Marquis of Carabas." And he led the King's party to the ballroom where the servants, happy to be rid of the horrible wizard, had prepared a great feast. The King was so impressed with the handsome young Marquis that he offered him his daughter's hand in marriage. They were married that very afternoon. And at their castle, Puss had a special place of honor and they all lived happily ever after.

Sleeping Beauty

Long ago there lived a King and Queen who wished more than anything to have a child of their own. Many years passed and, at last, a beautiful baby girl was born. The King and Queen rejoiced

and planned a christening to celebrate. All the fairies
in the kingdom were invited—all but one. The King
forgot to include one of the oldest and most power-
ful fairies in the land. During the festivities, each

fairy bestowed a magic gift upon the little Princess. One gave her beauty, another, wisdom, a third, charm. Suddenly the fairy who had not been invited burst into the room. Angry at being neglected, her heart was filled with vengeance. Instead of bringing a gift to the baby, she brought a curse. "When the Princess is fifteen years old, she shall prick her finger on a spindle and die!" she shouted bitterly. She turned and left the castle without uttering another word.

There was still one fairy who had not yet presented her gift to the Princess. She stepped forward and told the grief-stricken King and Queen, "I cannot lift the curse placed on your child, but I can use my special power to alter it. The Princess shall not die. She and everyone in the castle shall fall into a deep sleep which will last 100 years and then she will be awakened by the son of a King."

But the royal couple was not consoled. Desperate to protect their precious child, the King ordered his servants to gather and burn every spindle in the kingdom.

As the Princess grew, the promises of the fairies' blessings came true. She was certainly lovely and wise, as well as kind and cheerful. It so happened that on her fifteenth birthday, the lovely Princess was wandering through the great castle exploring unfamiliar rooms. High in a tower she had never

seen she discovered a strange room. There sat a wrinkled old woman busily spinning. The Princess, having never seen a spinning wheel before, was fascinated. "May I try?" she asked. As soon as her

hand touched the spindle, pricking her finger, the
fairy's curse came true. Everyone in the castle fell
right to sleep. A thick hedge of rose briars grew
up around the castle and a legend spread about the

beautiful sleeping Princess. Although brave men tried, no one ever conquered the jungle of brambles and weeds. One hundred years passed and a King's son traveling through the land heard the story of the

sleeping Princess. He sought the wall of thorns prepared to fight his way through. But the brambles parted and let him pass. The castle was haunted with a terrible silence, but the Prince searched until he found the Princess. He stared in wonder at her beauty, still fresh and lovely. His heart filled with love and he gently kissed her. At the touch of his lips, the spell was broken! The Princess opened her eyes and the castle came to life! The good fairy's blessing came true. The King and Queen were so happy for their daughter. A grand wedding was planned and everyone from the whole countryside was invited. And after the ceremony there was a wonderful celebration with tables laden with food. The Prince and Princess enjoyed a long and happy life together, beginning that very day.

Cinderella

Once there was a nobleman who, after his wife died, married a proud and cruel woman. She had two daughters who were just like her and very plain. The nobleman had a daughter, too, who was kind and sweet and very beautiful. Her stepmother was jealous of her beauty and so always treated her unfairly. Dressed in rags, the girl worked as a servant in the house and slept in the kitchen by the fireplace. And so her name became Cinderella.

One day the King's son gave a grand ball and the stepsisters were invited. They were so excited! Cinderella worked harder than ever to prepare their gowns and hair so they would look beautiful. Poor Cinderella! She dreamed of going to the ball, but the nasty sisters only laughed and sneered, "Surely, you can't be serious! The Prince would never look at you in those rags."

At last the day came and Cinderella watched sadly as the two plain sisters, dressed all in silks and satin, set out for the ball. Then she sat down beside the cold hearth and cried. She wanted so much to be able to go to the ball.

Suddenly she heard a noise. Startled, Cinderella looked up with wide eyes. Beside her on the hearth stood a funny little woman with sparkling blue eyes. "Who are you?" Cinderella asked quickly.

"I'm your fairy godmother," said the old woman smiling gently. "Now tell me why you are crying." But Cinderella could not speak. "You want to go to the ball, I know," the old woman said, "and so you shall! First, run into the garden and get me the largest pumpkin." Cinderella was so astonished she ran and did as she was told. She brought her fairy godmother a pumpkin and then a mouse trap with six little mice, and a rat trap with a fat, round rat, and finally six lizards. Then her fairy godmother waved her magic wand and the pumpkin became

a golden coach. The mice turned into six magnificent horses. The rat changed into a fat, jolly coachman and the lizards stood as six fully dressed footmen. "Now you are ready to go to the ball."

"But," Cinderella stammered, "what about these rags?" Her fairy godmother did not answer but waved her wonderful wand. As Cinderella looked up a gown of gold and silver with beautiful ruffles was gently floating down toward her from a nearby tree. And then her fairy godmother gave her one more thing—a pair of tiny glass slippers, the prettiest in the world. Cinderella slipped them on and felt as light as air.

As Cinderella stepped into the coach, her fairy

godmother said, "You mustn't forget one thing. Do not stay past midnight, for when the hour strikes, everything will return to the way it was before."

"I promise," Cinderella said, and she set out for the ball full of joy.

At the palace, there was a hush when Cinderella entered the great ballroom. Everyone admired her beauty and wondered who the mysterious Princess was. The King's son, the handsome Prince, greeted her and asked her to dance. All evening he danced only with Cinderella. He was overwhelmed by this beautiful girl who moved gracefully in his arms. As they danced, he fell in love and never wanted to let her go.

Cinderella was so happy she forgot her fairy godmother's warning. Suddenly, through the music, she heard the palace clock striking the hour of twelve. She fled from the ballroom and down the palace steps. Hurrying, she lost one of her glass slippers. When the Prince tried to follow her, all he found was the little slipper. His guards saw nothing but a poor young girl in ragged work clothes.

The Prince was determined to search the country to find the mysterious girl who had captured his heart. He sent out a proclamation that he would marry the girl who could wear the tiny glass slipper. The Prince's messengers took the slipper to every house in the kingdom, instructed to try it on

every girl. When they came to the house of the two sisters, each tried to force her foot into the slipper but neither could get the shoe on.

Cinderella came forward in her dirty rags and shyly asked, "May I try on the slipper?" Her step-sisters laughed cruelly but the royal messenger agreed. To the amazement of everyone, the slipper fit her small foot perfectly. And at that moment, her fairy godmother appeared. She tapped Cinderella on the shoulder changing her rags into a gown even more splendid than the one she wore to the ball. And so, Cinderella was taken in the royal coach to the Prince at the palace. They were married in the most glorious celebration the kingdom had ever seen. And they lived happily ever after.

The Musicians of Bremen

Not far from Bremen there was a donkey whose job, for many years, was to pull heavy loads of corn to the mill for his cruel master. But the donkey was getting old now—his step was slow and he could no longer carry such heavy loads. The donkey knew that his master wanted to get rid of him so, rather than wait for his fate, he ran away. He set out for the town of Bremen. "My voice is still strong," he thought to himself, "so I will look for work as a town musician."

On his way he met a dog lying beside the road. "What is the matter?" the donkey asked.

"I used to be a hunting dog, but now I am old. My legs will not go swiftly and my nose is not so keen and now my master wants to be rid of me," the hound answered pitifully.

"Why not join me?" the donkey said. "If you are a hunting dog I am sure you have a fine howl." And so the two set out together.

Soon they came upon a cat sitting miserably by the road. "Are you lost?" asked the donkey.

"I do not know what to do," said the cat. "I am old and tired and my mistress says a cat who cannot catch mice does not earn his keep, so I had to leave my home."

"Well," said the donkey, "you must come with us to Bremen where we are to be town musicians. If you are a cat who sings to the moon, I am sure you have a fine, high voice."

So the three friends trotted merrily along the road to Bremen. Soon they came upon a farm where a rooster was perched on a gate crowing loudly. "What a voice!" exclaimed the donkey. "But why do you crow when the sun is setting?"

"It is my last chance," the rooster cried. "I am crowing my loudest because tomorrow the farmer's wife is putting me in a soup."

"Oh, my," said the donkey. "You had better come

with us. We are going to Bremen to be town musicians." So the four friends went down the road as
the sun began to set. But Bremen was still far away
when the cold night fell. They had to look for a

place to spend the night. So the rooster flew to the top of a tree and looked around.

"I see a light," he called. "It might be a house where we could be warm." So they went toward the

light and, indeed, it was a small house. The donkey, who was the tallest, crept up and peered in the window.

"What do you see?" asked the cat.

"What do I see? Oh-h I see a band of robbers seated at a table laden with food! And never have I seen such rich and glorious looking food. Oh-h I'm so hungry." The robbers were also surrounded by stolen gold and jewels. And a warm fire glowed in the fireplace.

The four friends knew they wanted to go in to the house for the night, but how were they going to get the robbers to leave? They moved away from the house to decide on a plan.

"No one of us alone could scare those robbers," said the donkey, "but if we all work together we might be able to."

"Well," said the cat, "I remember once, a long time ago, my mother told me . . . . "

The animals listened very carefully to the cat's story. Then they went quietly back to the window. They knew their plan would work. The donkey stood on his hind legs and placed his hooves on the sill. The dog jumped on his back and the cat leapt onto the dog. The rooster flew up and perched on the cat's head. And then the donkey brayed, the dog howled, the cat meowed and the rooster crowed louder than ever before! What a noise! Terrified, the robbers burst out the door and fled into the woods.

The four new friends ate and drank heartily and complimented each other on their fine plan. They

never gave a moments thought to the robbers for the rest of the evening. Happy with their cozy home for the night, they went to sleep. The donkey found a bed of straw in the backyard. The dog lay behind the door. The cat curled up by the fireplace and the rooster flew up on a high beam.

But the robbers, who were waiting not far away, then realized that all was quiet. They decided to sneak back to the house. They were hungry and wanted to finish the delicious meal. One stealthily entered the house and went to the dying fire. When he leaned down to fan the coals, the cat leapt into his face hissing and scratching. He ran screaming to the door and tripped over the dog who bit his leg.

Rushing into the yard, he ran into the donkey who kicked him with all his might. The rooster awoke and crowed a terrible chorus of "cock-a-doodle-dos." The robber, shaking with fright, ran to the others

and told them, "That place is full of monsters. Run as fast as you can!" So the robbers left the house to the four musicians who stayed on living and singing joyfully to the end of their days.